Money Magnet

Harness the Power of Positive Thinking and Transformative Habits to Attract Financial Success

Happy Wynn

ISBN: 9798391255659

Imprint: Independently published

Cover design by: Echo Enterprise LLC.

Library of Congress Control Number: 2018675309

Printed in the United States of America

DISCLAIMER

The information provided in this book is intended for educational and informational purposes only and does not constitute professional advice or treatment. It is not a substitute for the advice of a qualified professional.

Please be aware that the author and publisher of this book are not medical, legal, financial, or mental health professionals and do not provide any medical, legal, mental health, or financial advice. Readers should rely on the information presented in this book at their own risk.

While every effort has been made to ensure the accuracy, reliability, and completeness of the information contained in this book, the author and publisher make no representations or warranties, express or implied, about the suitability or availability of the information. The information is provided on an "as is" basis, and the author and publisher will not be held liable for any loss, injury, or damage arising directly or indirectly from the use or application of the information contained in this book.

It is important to recognize that each individual's circumstances and experiences are unique. Therefore, the strategies and methods presented in this book may not be effective for everyone. The author and publisher do not guarantee any specific results or success from following the advice in this book.

If you require professional medical, legal, financial, or mental health advice or treatment, please consult a qualified professional. The author and publisher of this book disclaim any responsibility for any adverse effects that may result from the use or application of the information contained in this book. Use it at your own risk.

By choosing to purchase or read this book, you agree to indemnify and absolve the author, publisher, and any other associated parties from any liability arising from errors, omissions, inaccuracies, or misrepresentations. It is important to acknowledge that web-linked content may change over time, and certain events may have been modified. Some events are based on the author's current recollections of experiences throughout their life. The author and publisher offer no guarantees or warranties in relation to the information provided within the book.

Table of Contents

INTRODUCTION

In today's society, financial success is frequently regarded as a primary measure of personal achievement and contentment. The pursuit of financial freedom, however, can be intimidating and seemingly unattainable for many. Nevertheless, by tapping into the potential of positive thinking and altering your habits, you can become a money magnet, attracting financial prosperity into your life.

This book chronicles my personal journey of overcoming financial hurdles and attaining financial abundance. Throughout my life, I have experienced both the highs and lows of financial stability. Following my college graduation, I easily earned money and enjoyed a comfortable lifestyle. This changed when I became involved with a significant other who possessed a pessimistic, skeptical, doubtful, and unmotivated mindset. Gradually, his negative habits and beliefs undermined my confidence, motivation, and happiness, ultimately leading to the loss of everything I had worked for and plunging me into debt.

In the wake of our separation, I was heartbroken and despondent. It seemed as though I had reached my lowest point, devoid of hope for the future. Yet, I resolved to take control of my life and make a change. I began meditating, praying, and reevaluating my life, recognizing the need to modify my mindset and habits in order to achieve financial success and happiness. I surrounded myself with positive, supportive individuals who shared my aspirations and dreams. I also sought knowledge through books, podcasts, and videos on personal finance and investing. As a result, I learned to establish clear financial objectives, budget my money, save and invest wisely, and constantly enhance my skills and understanding.

As I altered my mindset and habits, I observed a corresponding improvement in my life. Money began to flow into my life effortlessly. I managed to eliminate my debt, grow my income, amass wealth, and ultimately achieve financial freedom. Simultaneously, I experienced greater happiness, health, and fulfillment in every aspect of my life. In this book, I aim to impart the principles and strategies that facilitated my transformation from financial despair to abundance. The lessons and strategies you will acquire are grounded in the real-world experiences of myself and others who have attained financial success by embracing these principles.

This book serves as an all-encompassing guide that will enable you to shift your mindset, nurture the appropriate habits, and ultimately become a money magnet. The book is divided into several sections, each concentrating on a crucial element of the journey towards financial success. Initially, we will explore the power of positive thinking and its capacity to enhance your confidence, motivation, creativity, and performance in the pursuit of your financial goals. We will examine key concepts of positive thinking, such as optimism, gratitude, resilience, and self-belief, while providing practical strategies for cultivating a positive mindset, including affirmations, positive self-talk, and visualization.

Subsequently, we will delve into transformative habits that pave the way for financial abundance. We will address essential habits, such as setting clear financial goals, budgeting and tracking expenses, saving and investing, and continuous learning and self-improvement. Additionally, we will offer strategies for developing and maintaining these habits, such as starting small, creating routines and schedules, and utilizing rewards and incentives.

Furthermore, we will discuss the significance of networking and mentorship in attracting financial success. We will propose strategies for constructing a network of accomplished individuals who can offer guidance, support, and inspiration throughout your financial journey. We will also share insights on how to identify mentors capable of imparting valuable lessons from their own experiences.

Moreover, we will tackle overcoming financial obstacles, providing strategies for resilience and adaptability in the face of setbacks. We will explore coping with stress, uncertainty, and failure while maintaining a positive outlook. We will also share stories of individuals who have triumphed over financial challenges by employing positive thinking and transformative habits.

Lastly, we will present inspiring case studies of individuals who have become money magnets by implementing these principles and strategies. We will showcase their stories of financial success and happiness, emphasizing their mindset, habits, and actions that enabled them to achieve their goals.

Upon completing this book, you will possess a profound understanding of the mindset and habits necessary to attract financial success. You will be equipped with practical strategies to transform your thinking, develop positive habits, and become a money magnet. Embark on this exciting journey and unlock your potential for financial abundance.

Money Magnet

By Melody Wallack

*I*n the realm where mindset shapes our fate,
A Money Magnet stands at destiny's gate.
With thoughts of abundance, success in the air,
Prosperity blossoms, as dreams become clear.

*T*ransformative habits, the compass we steer,
Foundations of wealth, as we conquer our fears.
Saving and investing, learning each day,
The Money Magnet's power guides our way.

*S*trategic connections, mentors to find,
A network of wisdom, as stars align.
For wealth is a journey, a dance, a pursuit,
With resilience and courage, our dreams take root.

*T*hrough setbacks and challenges, we rise and we grow,
The Money Magnet's strength, a beacon that glows.
Embracing the long-term, the future in sight,
Financial success, our birthright, our right.

$\mathcal{M}$oney Magnet, a force that attracts,
Prosperity, abundance, the wealth we enact.
For in this dance of life, our goals we pursue,
The Money Magnet within, forever shines true.

Chapter 1

The Power of Positive Thinking

A. Understanding Positive Thinking

Definition and Key Concepts

Do you aspire to live a happier, healthier, and more successful life? If so, consider initiating a change in your mindset. Positive thinking is more than a mere buzzword or passing trend; it is a potent tool that can transform your life for the better.

Positive thinking involves focusing on life's brighter aspects and maintaining an optimistic outlook. It entails searching for the silver lining in challenging situations, embracing hope, and having faith in one's abilities to overcome obstacles. By adopting a positive mindset, you can enhance your overall well-being, boost self-confidence, and foster a greater sense of happiness and fulfillment.

Key concepts of positive thinking include:

• *Optimism*: Holding a belief in favorable outcomes and anticipating the best possible results. Optimism can help you cope with stress, reduce anxiety, and increase motivation.

• *Gratitude*: Recognizing and appreciating life's blessings, regardless of their magnitude. Gratitude can help you cultivate positive emotions, strengthen your relationships, and heighten your satisfaction with life.

• *Resilience*: Recovering from setbacks and utilizing them as opportunities for growth. Resilience can assist you in overcoming challenges, learning from failures, and adapting to changing circumstances.

• *Self-belief*: Having faith in your abilities and talents to achieve your goals and dreams. Self-belief can bolster your self-esteem, enable you to pursue your passions, and unlock your potential.

Benefits of Positive Thinking in Various Aspects of Life

Positive thinking has been associated with numerous benefits across diverse facets of life, including:

• *Improved mental and physical health:* Research indicates that positive thinkers tend to possess more robust immune systems, lower stress levels, better mental health, reduced depression rates, superior pain tolerance, and a decreased risk of death from cardiovascular disease, stroke, cancer, respiratory conditions, and infections. Positive thinking can also help prevent or manage chronic illnesses such as diabetes, hypertension, and arthritis.

➢ In **a study conducted by Lisa R. Yanek**, M.P.H., and her colleagues at Johns Hopkins, individuals with a family history of heart disease who maintained a positive outlook were found to be one-third less likely to experience a heart attack or other cardiovascular events within five to 25 years compared to those with more negative outlooks. The study also discovered that positive individuals from the general population had a 13% lower likelihood of having a heart attack or other coronary events than their negative counterparts.

➢ **A study by Mental Health Matters** demonstrated that positive thinking has a significant impact on physical and emotional health. Positive thinking has been shown to reduce stress, improve overall health, increase life expectancy, and bolster our ability to cope with adversity.

➢ **A study by Light Warriors Legion** summarized several scientific investigations on positive thinking, finding that it offers advantages such as reducing the risk of heart attacks, improving immune system function, increasing pain tolerance, enhancing creativity and problem-solving skills, and boosting self-confidence and happiness.

➢ **A study by Dr. Kiltz** underscored the benefits of positive thinking for various aspects of life, including mental and physical health, relationships, career, finances, spirituality, and personal growth4. The study also provided quotes and techniques to help cultivate a positive mindset.

- *Greater success in personal and professional pursuits:* An optimistic outlook can help you maintain motivation, persistence, and focus on your goals. Research has also found that positive thinking can enhance creativity, problem-solving skills, and performance. Positive thinkers are more likely to achieve their objectives, earn higher incomes, and advance in their careers.

- *Enhanced relationships:* Positive thinking can foster better communication, understanding, and empathy, which can improve relationships with family, friends, and colleagues. Positive thinkers are more likely to attract and maintain positive social support, which can buffer them from stress and loneliness.

- *Increased happiness and life satisfaction:* A positive mindset can help you derive more enjoyment and satisfaction from everyday experiences. Positive thinkers also tend to have higher self-esteem, greater optimism, and fewer negative emotions. They are more likely to experience positive emotions such as joy, love, and gratitude, which can improve their mood and well-being.

B. The Relationship between Positive Thinking and Financial Success

How Self-Belief and Visualization Can Boost Your Finances

One of the critical factors influencing your financial success is your mindset. A positive mindset entails believing in yourself and your ability to achieve your financial goals. It also involves using visualization to create a clear and vivid image of what you want to accomplish and how you will get there. **For example**, envisioning yourself debt-free and setting up a detailed plan to pay off your debt can make you feel motivated and empowered to take the necessary steps.

Similarly, picturing yourself as a homeowner or enjoying a vacation in Hawaii can inspire you to save diligently and make wise investment decisions to turn those dreams into reality. By maintaining a positive outlook and focusing on achievable milestones, you can overcome obstacles and work towards a more secure financial future.

Self-belief and visualization are potent tools that can help you shape your reality and attract wealth and abundance. When you believe in yourself, you act with confidence and conviction. You don't let fear or doubt prevent you from pursuing your passions and taking calculated risks. You also attract positive people and opportunities that support your goals and vision.

Visualization aids in programming your subconscious mind to align with your conscious desires. By regularly visualizing your financial goals, you activate the law of attraction, which posits that you attract what you focus on. You also stimulate the creative part of your brain, which helps you generate ideas and solutions for achieving your goals.

How to Overcome Self-Limiting Beliefs that Hold You Back

One of the most significant obstacles to financial success is self-limiting beliefs. These negative thoughts and assumptions about yourself, your abilities, and your possibilities can limit your potential and sabotage your efforts to improve your financial situation.

Some common self-limiting beliefs that can affect your finances are:

- I don't deserve wealth or abundance.
- I'm not good enough or smart enough to be financially successful.
- Money is the root of all evil, or money corrupts people.

- Financial success is only for the lucky or privileged few.

Positive thinking can help you overcome these self-limiting beliefs and replace them with empowering ones. By changing the way you think about yourself and money, you can alter the way you feel and act. Consequently, you can change the results you get.

To overcome self-limiting beliefs, you need to:

> **Identify them**: Become aware of the negative thoughts that run through your mind and how they affect your emotions and behavior. In this case, you need to recognize the negative thoughts that are holding you back from starting your own business and understand how they're impacting your confidence and motivation.

> **Challenge them**: Question the validity and accuracy of these thoughts and look for evidence that contradicts them. Ask yourself if these thoughts are based on facts or if they're just assumptions or opinions. Look for examples of successful entrepreneurs who started with little experience or skills and learn from their stories. Seek feedback from people who believe in you and your potential to start your own business.

> **Replace them**: Create positive affirmations that reflect the truth about yourself and your potential. Repeat them daily until they become ingrained in your mind. **Examples** of positive affirmations could be "*I have the creativity and resourcefulness to start*

and grow my own business" or *"I am capable of overcoming challenges and achieving success as an entrepreneur."* By focusing on these positive affirmations, you can reprogram your mind to believe in your potential and take action towards your goal of starting your own business.

Here are some examples for each step:

Identify them:

"I'm not good enough to apply for that job."

"I'm not talented enough to pursue my dreams."

"I'm not smart enough to succeed."

Challenge them:

"Is it really true that I'm not good enough, or am I just believing that because of past failures or criticism?"

"What evidence do I have that supports the idea that I'm not talented enough? What evidence contradicts that belief?"

"Have I always been unsuccessful, or are there times when I've accomplished something I thought I couldn't?"

Replace them:

"I have valuable skills and experiences that make me a strong candidate for this job."

"My talents and passions are unique and can help me achieve my dreams."

"I am intelligent and capable of learning new things and achieving success."

To overcome self-limiting beliefs and achieve financial success, you need to take control of your thoughts and cultivate a positive mindset. Start by identifying the negative thoughts that hold you back and recognizing how they impact your emotions and behavior. This awareness is the first step towards challenging and replacing them with positive, empowering beliefs.

When you catch yourself thinking negatively, pause and question the validity and accuracy of these thoughts. Look for evidence that contradicts them, and remind yourself of your strengths, accomplishments, and potential. Don't let self-doubt and fear hold you back from pursuing your financial goals.

To reinforce your positive mindset, create affirmations that reflect the truth about yourself and your potential. Repeat them daily, preferably in front of a mirror, until they become ingrained in your mind. Some examples of affirmations include "*I am worthy of financial abundance*," "*I have the skills and knowledge to succeed*," and "*I am open to new opportunities and experiences*."

Remember, changing your thoughts and beliefs takes time and effort. Be patient, persistent, and consistent in your practice. With dedication and the right mindset, you can overcome self-limiting beliefs and achieve the financial success you desire.

C. Strategies to Develop a Positive Mindset

1. How to Use Affirmations and Positive Self-Talk to Boost Your Finances

Cultivating a positive mindset can be achieved through the use of affirmations and positive self-talk. These techniques help reshape your thoughts and emotions about yourself and your financial situation, leading to transformative outcomes.

a) Affirmations

Affirmations are positive statements that reinforce your desired beliefs and outcomes. They help replace self-limiting beliefs with empowering thoughts that shape your mindset and behavior. To create effective affirmations, follow these guidelines:

- *Be specific*: Clearly state your desired outcome or feeling. **Example**: Instead of saying, "*I want to be successful*," say, "*I am a successful entrepreneur with a thriving business.*"

- *Use present tense*: Phrase your affirmation as if you already possess or embody the desired quality. **Example**: Instead of saying, "*I will be confident,*" say, "*I am confident in my abilities and decisions.*" Instead of saying, "*I will pass my nursing board exam,*" say, "*I pass my nursing board exam.*" Instead of saying, "*I will be a millionaire,*" say, "*I am a millionaire.*"

- **Stay positive**: Avoid negative terms like "not" or "don't" and focus on desired outcomes instead of unwanted ones. **Example**: Instead of saying, *"I don't want to be stressed,"* say, *"I am calm and in control of my emotions."*

- **Evoke emotion**: Include words that elicit positive emotions such as *"happy", "grateful", or "confident"*. **Example**: Instead of saying, *"I am successful,"* say, *"I am grateful for my achievements and the opportunities that come my way."*

Integrate affirmations into your daily routine by repeating them aloud or in your mind, writing them down, displaying them in visible locations, or listening to them as audio recordings.

b) Positive Self-Talk

Positive self-talk involves replacing negative thoughts with positive, supportive ones. Negative thoughts can erode your confidence, motivation, and happiness, and even create a self-fulfilling prophecy where you expect and attract more negativity into your life.

Develop a more optimistic outlook by practicing positive self-talk. When you notice negative thoughts, pause and reframe the thought into a more constructive and encouraging statement.

Here are some examples of financial affirmations:

- "I am deserving of financial abundance."

- "I am capable of managing and growing my wealth."
- "Money flows effortlessly into my life."
- "I am grateful for all the opportunities and resources that come my way."
- "I am confident and successful in my financial endeavors."

To better illustrate the concept of positive self-talk, here is a table of examples of negative thoughts and their positive self-talk alternatives:

Negative Thought	Positive Self-Talk
I'll never be able to pay off my debt.	I am taking steps to reduce my debt and improve my financial situation.
I'm not good enough to earn more money.	I have valuable skills and talents that I can use to increase my income.
I always make bad financial decisions.	I learn from my mistakes and make better choices in the future.
I can't stick to a budget.	I am committed to creating and following a budget that suits my needs.
Saving money is impossible for me.	I will find ways to save money, even if it's a small amount at a time.

Negative Thought	Positive Self-Talk
I'll never achieve my financial goals.	I am setting realistic financial goals and working towards them every day.
Investing is too risky and complicated for me	I will educate myself on investing and make informed decisions to grow my wealth.
I can't negotiate for a better salary.	I will prepare and confidently ask for the salary I deserve during negotiations.
Financial success is only for the lucky few.	Financial success is achievable through hard work, planning, and persistence.
I'll never be able to retire comfortably.	I am taking action now to ensure a secure and comfortable retirement.

By consistently using affirmations and positive self-talk, whether through daily journaling or the use of affirmation apps, you will develop a positive mindset that empowers you to achieve your financial goals and aspirations.

With so many free apps available for download, it's easy to set and customize your affirmations, and receive regular reminders to stay on track. By taking advantage of these resources, you can strengthen your positive thinking and create a mental environment that fosters financial success.

How to Surround Yourself with Positivity and Gratitude

Your environment and the people around you can significantly impact your mindset, either lifting you up or dragging you down. To cultivate a positive mindset, it's essential to immerse yourself in positivity and gratitude.

A. Surrounding Yourself with Positivity

Positivity, the quality of being optimistic, hopeful, and cheerful, can help you cope with stress, overcome challenges, and achieve your goals. To surround yourself with positivity:

- *Seek out positive and supportive people* who believe in your financial goals and dreams. These individuals encourage you, celebrate your successes, and offer constructive feedback. They can be family, friends, mentors, or peers. Join online communities or groups that share your interests and aspirations.
- *Consume uplifting content, such as books, podcasts, and videos* that inspire and motivate you to pursue financial success. These sources provide valuable insights, tips, and stories to help you learn and grow. Follow positive influencers or role models who have achieved financial success and happiness.
- *Limit exposure to negativity, including negative people and media* that foster pessimism or self-doubt. Avoid individuals who criticize, discourage, or sabotage your efforts. These can be toxic relatives, friends, coworkers, or strangers. Steer clear of media that promotes fear,

anger, or sadness, such as certain news outlets, social media platforms, or shows that trigger negative emotions.

B. Practicing Gratitude

Gratitude, the quality of being thankful and appreciative, shifts your focus from what you lack to what you already have. This shift in perspective cultivates a positive mindset and improves overall well-being. To practice gratitude:

- *Keep a daily gratitude journal*, listing things you are thankful for each day. These can be big or small things that make you happy or improve your life. For example, you can be grateful for your health, your family, your income, or even a sunny day.
- *Express gratitude towards others*, acknowledging their kindness and support. You can do this by saying thank you verbally or in writing, giving compliments or gifts, or returning favors. Show gratitude by being generous and helpful to others in need.
- *Regularly reflect on your accomplishments and progress*, appreciating the journey towards financial success. Review your goals and achievements periodically, celebrate your milestones and wins, and learn from your failures and setbacks.

By incorporating these strategies into your daily routine, you can develop a positive mindset that supports your journey to financial abundance. This optimistic outlook will empower you to overcome self-limiting beliefs, maintain motivation, and ultimately attract financial success.

"Sow a thought, reap an action; sow an action, reap a habit; sow a habit, reap a character; sow a character, reap a destiny."

-This quote is often attributed to various authors, including Ralph Waldo Emerson, Charles Reade, and Stephen R. Covey.

Positive Thinking

By Melody Wallack

In the garden of the mind, where thoughts gently sway,

A seed of hope is planted, a beacon to light the way.

With every dream envisioned, a tapestry we weave,

Positive thinking, the key, as we dare to believe.

Amidst the storms of doubt, in the shadows of despair,

A ray of sunlight beckons, a whisper in the air.

For every challenge conquered, every fear set free

The power of positive thinking shapes our destiny.

A fortress of optimism, our thoughts a shield we wield,

As we march toward our goals, refusing to yield.

In this dance of life, where our dreams take flight,

The beauty of believing ignites the night.

With every step we take, each milestone we greet,

The magic of positive thinking makes us complete.

For in the depths of our soul, our hearts do know,

The strength we possess, as we continue to grow.

So let us rejoice in the power, the beauty, the grace,

Of positive thinking, as we find our place.

For when we dare to believe, to dream, to aspire,

We light up the world, with our hearts on fire.

Chapter 2

Transformative Habits for Financial Success

A. The Importance of Habits in Achieving Financial Success

Habits are the small, repeated actions that shape our daily lives and ultimately determine our long-term success. When it comes to financial success, cultivating the right habits is crucial, as they help you manage your money effectively, make wise decisions, and stay on track to achieve your financial goals. In this section, we will explore key habits for financial success and provide strategies for building and maintaining them.

B. Key Habits for Financial Success

1. Setting Clear Financial Goals: Setting clear and specific financial goals is the first step towards achieving financial success. These goals provide direction and motivation, guiding your financial decisions and habits. To set effective financial goals:

- Make them **SMART**: Specific, Measurable, Achievable, Relevant, and Time-bound. **For example**, instead of saying *"I want to save more money"*, say *"I want to save $10,000 in one year for a down payment on a house"*.

- Break larger goals into smaller, manageable milestones. **For example**, if your goal is to save $10,000 in one year, break it down into monthly or weekly targets.
- Regularly review and adjust your goals as needed. Monitor your progress and celebrate your achievements. If you encounter challenges or changes in your circumstances, revise your goals accordingly.

2. Budgeting and Tracking Expenses: Creating and maintaining a budget is a fundamental habit for financial success. A budget helps you understand your income and expenses, allowing you to make informed decisions and allocate resources effectively. To create a budget:

- *List all sources of income and monthly expenses.* Include fixed expenses (e.g., rent, utilities) and variable expenses (e.g., groceries, clothing).

- *Categorize your expenses* into essential (e.g., housing, food) and discretionary (e.g., entertainment, dining out) spending. Essential expenses are those necessary for your survival and well-being. Discretionary expenses are those that are optional or non-essential.

- *Set spending limits* for each category and track your expenses to ensure you stay within those limits. You can use apps or tools such as Mint or YNAB to help you track your spending. Ideally, you should spend less than you earn and allocate some money for savings and investments.

3. Saving and Investing: Saving and investing are essential habits for building wealth and achieving financial success. They involve setting aside a portion of your income for future use, either in a savings account or through investments that can generate additional income. To save and invest effectively:

- **Pay yourself first.** This means setting aside a percentage of your income for savings or investments before spending on anything else. You can automate this process by setting up direct deposits or transfers from your paycheck or bank account to your savings or investment account.

- **Choose the right savings or investment option for your goals and risk tolerance.** There are various options available such as savings accounts, certificates of deposit (CDs), stocks, bonds, mutual funds, etc. Each option has different features such as interest rates, returns, fees, risks, liquidity, etc. Conduct research and consult a financial advisor if needed to find the best option for you.

- **Diversify your portfolio.** This means spreading your money across different types of investments to reduce risk and increase returns. For example, you can invest in a mix of stocks, bonds, and cash equivalents to balance risk and reward.

4. Continuous Learning and Self-Improvement: Financial success requires ongoing learning and self-improvement. Staying informed about personal finance topics and refining your money management skills can help you make better decisions and achieve your financial goals. To cultivate a habit of continuous learning:

- **Read books, articles, and blogs** on personal finance and investing. Some examples are The Richest Man in

Babylon by George S. Clason, Rich Dad Poor Dad by Robert Kiyosaki, The Total Money Makeover by Dave Ramsey, The Intelligent Investor by Benjamin Graham, etc.

- *Attend workshops, seminars, and online courses* to deepen your financial knowledge. Some examples are Financial Peace University by Dave Ramsey, Personal Finance 101 by Coursera, Investing 101 by Udemy, etc.

- *Seek advice from financial experts and mentors.* You can find them online or offline through platforms such as NerdWallet, Investopedia, BiggerPockets, etc. Don't hesitate to ask questions and learn from their experiences and insights.

5. Building and Maintaining a Strong Financial Network: Surrounding yourself with like-minded individuals who share your financial goals can help you stay motivated and learn new strategies for financial success. A strong financial network can provide support, advice, and opportunities. To build and maintain a strong financial network:

- *Join local or online financial communities*, such as personal finance forums, social media groups, or investment clubs. Engage in discussions, share your experiences, and learn from others' perspectives.

- *Attend networking events and conferences* focused on personal finance, investing, and wealth-building. These events can help you meet professionals and experts in the field, as well as make connections with other individuals who share your financial goals.

- *Maintain relationships with your financial network* by regularly checking in, sharing updates, and providing support. A strong network can offer encouragement, accountability, and valuable advice.

By incorporating these transformative habits into your daily routine, you can pave the way for financial success and achieve your financial goals more efficiently. Remember that building habits takes time and effort, so be patient and stay committed to your journey towards financial freedom.

Transformative Habits for Financial Success

Chapter 3

Attracting Financial Success through Networking

A. The Power of Networking and Connections

Networking is one of the most effective ways to attract financial success, as it allows you to tap into the knowledge, experience, and opportunities of successful individuals in your field. According to a study by LinkedIn, 85% of jobs are filled through networking[12]. Networking can also help you establish your reputation, credibility, and influence in your industry, which can lead to more referrals, clients, and partnerships. In this section, we will discuss why networking is so important for attracting financial success, and how you can build and maintain a network of successful people who can support you in your journey.

Some of the benefits of networking for financial success include:

- **Learning from others:** Networking can help you learn from the successes and failures of others who have achieved financial success. You can gain valuable insights, advice, and feedback from them that can help you improve your skills, strategies, and mindset. You can also access resources and information that can help you stay updated on the latest trends, opportunities, and challenges in your field.

- *Accessing opportunities*: Networking can help you access opportunities that can accelerate your financial success. You can find out about new projects, investments, collaborations, or job openings that match your interests and goals. You can also leverage your network to introduce you to potential clients, partners, mentors, or investors who can help you grow your business or career.

- *Establishing reputation*: Networking can help you establish your reputation as a trustworthy, competent, and reliable professional in your field. You can showcase your expertise, achievements, and values to your network and beyond. You can also build trust and rapport with your network by providing value, support, and referrals to them. By doing so, you can increase your visibility and influence in your industry and attract more opportunities.

B. Strategies for Effective Networking

To make the most of networking opportunities and attract financial success, you should adopt the following strategies:

- **Be genuine and authentic**: When networking, be yourself and avoid trying to impress others with a façade. People are more likely to connect with and trust someone who is genuine and authentic. Share your true interests, passions, and goals, and listen actively to others to understand their perspectives.

- *Focus on building relationships:* Networking is not just about exchanging business cards or adding contacts on social media. It's about building meaningful, long-lasting relationships. Invest time and effort in getting to know people, understanding their needs, and finding ways to support and add value to them.

- *Attend industry events and conferences*: Participate in events and conferences related to your field or interests to meet like-minded professionals and potential partners. These events provide an excellent platform for networking, learning, and showcasing your expertise.

- *Join professional organizations and online communities*: Become a member of professional organizations or online communities related to your field to expand your network, access resources, and stay informed about industry trends and opportunities.

- *Follow up and stay in touch*: After meeting someone new, follow up with a message or email expressing your appreciation for the conversation and any relevant information or resources. Stay in touch with your contacts by sharing updates, asking for advice, or offering assistance. This helps to strengthen your relationships and maintain your network.

By adopting these strategies, you can build and maintain a strong network of successful individuals who can support and contribute to your financial success. Remember that networking is an ongoing process, and nurturing relationships takes time and effort. Stay committed to building and maintaining your network, and you will see the benefits of attracting financial success.

Some of the strategies for building and nurturing a network of successful people are:

- *Joining networking groups*: One of the easiest ways to start networking is to join groups that are relevant to your field or interests. These can be formal groups such as Business Networking International (BNI), which brings together professionals from different industries who share leads and referrals, or informal groups such as social media communities or online forums where you can interact with like-minded people. You can also join industry associations or events where you can meet and connect with influential people in your field.

- *Being proactive*: Another strategy for building a network is to be proactive in reaching out to people who you want to connect with. You can use platforms such as LinkedIn or Twitter to find and follow people who are successful in your field or niche. You can then engage with their content by liking, commenting, or sharing it. You can also send them personalized messages or emails expressing your interest in their work and asking for their advice or feedback. You can also ask for introductions from mutual contacts or referrals from existing connections.

- *Providing value*: A key strategy for nurturing a network is to provide value to your connections. This means offering something that is useful, relevant, or beneficial to them without expecting anything in return. **For example**, you can share helpful resources or information that they might need or appreciate. You can also give them compliments, testimonials, or recommendations that boost their reputation. You can also support them by attending their events, promoting their products or services, or referring them to potential clients or partners.

Some examples of successful networkers are:

- *Oprah Winfrey*: Oprah Winfrey is one of the most influential media personalities in the world who has built a vast network of successful people from various fields. She has used her network to create opportunities for herself and others by launching her own television network (OWN), magazine (O), book club (Oprah's Book Club), podcast (SuperSoul Conversations), and foundation (Oprah Winfrey Leadership Academy Foundation). She has also leveraged her network to support causes that she cares about such as education, women's empowerment, and health[28].

- *Richard Branson*: Richard Branson is one of the most successful entrepreneurs in the world who has founded over 400 companies under his Virgin Group brand. He has built a network of successful people from different industries such as music, aviation, space travel, telecommunications, health care, and hospitality. He has used his network to create innovative products and services that challenge the status quo and drive change.

- *Bill Gates*: Bill Gates is one of the richest and most philanthropic people in the world who has co-founded Microsoft and the Bill & Melinda Gates Foundation. He has built a network of successful people from various fields such as technology, business, science, education, and health. He has used his network to collaborate on projects and initiatives that aim to solve some of the world's biggest problems such as poverty, disease, climate change, and inequality.

- *Sheryl Sandberg:* Sheryl Sandberg is one of the most powerful women in tech who is the chief operating officer of Facebook and the founder of Lean In. She has built a network of successful people from various fields such as media, politics, academia, and social justice. She has used her network to advocate for women's leadership and empowerment in the workplace and society. She has also used her network to cope with personal challenges such as the loss of her husband and the pandemic.

C. Nurturing Relationships and Adding Value

Building a strong network is not just about making connections; it's about nurturing relationships and adding value to those connections. To strengthen your network, you should:

- *Offer support, advice, or resources* to help others in your network achieve their goals. **For example**, you can introduce them to someone who can help them with a challenge, recommend them for a job opportunity, or send them a book or a course that can improve their skills.

- *Share relevant articles, news, or events* with your connections to keep them informed and engaged. **For example**, you can forward them an article that relates to their interests, invite them to a webinar that covers a topic they are curious about, or tag them in a social media post that highlights their achievements.

- *Maintain regular contact* with your network, checking in periodically to stay updated on their progress and achievements. **For example**, you can send them a message or an email to ask how they are doing, congratulate them on a milestone, or wish them a happy birthday.

- *Be genuinely interested* in the success of others, celebrating their accomplishments and learning from their experiences. For example, you can give them positive feedback, testimonials, or endorsements that boost their reputation, express your appreciation and gratitude for their help or support, or ask them for advice or feedback on your own goals.

D. The Role of Mentorship in Financial Success

Mentorship can be a powerful catalyst for financial success. A mentor is an experienced individual who can provide guidance, advice, and support as you work towards your financial goals. Mentors can help you:

- **Identify areas of improvement** and develop strategies to address them. For example, a mentor can help you assess your strengths and weaknesses, set realistic and measurable goals or milestones, and create an action plan to achieve them.

- **Navigate challenges and setbacks** by sharing their own experiences and insights. For example, a mentor can help you overcome obstacles, learn from failures, and cope with stress by sharing their stories, lessons, and tips.

- **Stay accountable and focused** on your goals by providing encouragement and motivation. For example, a mentor can help you track your progress, celebrate your achievements, and remind you of your purpose and vision.

- **Expand your network** by introducing you to their connections and resources. For example, a mentor can help you access opportunities, referrals, partnerships, or investments by introducing you to their network of successful individuals.

To find a mentor, consider reaching out to successful individuals within your network or attending industry events and conferences. Express your interest in learning from their experiences and ask if they would be willing to provide guidance and support as you work towards your financial goals.

According to a study by KPMG, 28% of women who have mentors report having more confidence in their careers[14]. Another study by Sun Microsystems found that mentees were promoted five times more often than those without mentors[14]. Some examples of successful people who have benefited from mentorship are:

- *Mark Zuckerberg*: The founder and CEO of Facebook was mentored by Steve Jobs, the co-founder and former CEO of Apple. Jobs advised Zuckerberg on how to build a team, create a company culture, and focus on the long-term vision of Facebook.

- *Oprah Winfrey*: The media mogul was mentored by Maya Angelou, the renowned poet and author. Angelou inspired Winfrey with her wisdom, courage, and compassion. Winfrey said that Angelou was "one of the greatest influences of my entire life"[28].

- *Warren Buffett*: The billionaire investor was mentored by Benjamin Graham, the father of value investing. Graham taught Buffett how to analyze stocks, evaluate companies, and invest with discipline[6].

By leveraging the power of networking and mentorship, you can accelerate your progress towards financial success. Building a network of successful individuals can provide you with invaluable insights, resources, and opportunities, while mentorship can offer guidance and support as you navigate the challenges and setbacks that may arise along the way.

Chapter 4

Overcoming Financial Obstacles and Building Resilience

A. The Inevitability of Challenges and Setbacks

On the journey to financial success, you will inevitably face challenges and setbacks. Economic fluctuations, such as recessions or market crashes, unexpected expenses like medical emergencies or home repairs, or changes in personal circumstances due to job loss, health issues, or the death of a loved one can disrupt your plans and progress. Additionally, global events like the COVID-19 pandemic can have far-reaching financial impacts, affecting your income, investments, or even your overall financial stability. By cultivating resilience and adaptability, you can overcome these obstacles and continue moving towards your financial goals.

B. Building Resilience and Adaptability

Resilience is the ability to bounce back from adverse situations and cope with stress. Adaptability is the ability to adjust to changing conditions and find new ways to achieve your goals. These two qualities are essential for navigating financial challenges and setbacks. Here are some ways to build resilience and adaptability:

- *Embracing a growth mindset:* A growth mindset is the belief that abilities and intelligence can be developed through dedication and hard work. By adopting a growth mindset, you view challenges and setbacks as opportunities to learn and grow, rather than limitations. This mindset encourages you to persevere through difficulties and seek solutions to overcome obstacles. For example, instead of saying "*I can't do this*", you can say "*I can learn how to do this*".

- *Developing problem-solving skills*: Effective problem-solving skills are essential for finding creative and practical solutions to financial problems. To develop these skills:

  - Break down complex problems into smaller, more manageable components.
  - Identify the root causes of the problem and explore potential solutions.
  - Evaluate the pros and cons of each solution and choose the most appropriate course of action.
  - Regularly review and refine your problem-solving strategies to ensure they remain effective.

Case Study 1: Managing Debt

Jane is a 35-year-old single mother of two who is struggling with credit card debt. Her high-interest credit card balances have become unmanageable, and she is having difficulty making the minimum monthly payments. She decides to apply the problem-solving skills mentioned above.

1. *Break down complex problems*: Jane starts by listing her debts and categorizing them based on their interest rates and balances.
2. *Identify root causes and potential solutions*: She realizes that impulsive spending and lack of a proper budget have contributed to her debt. She explores solutions such as consolidating her debt, negotiating lower interest rates with her creditors, and creating a realistic budget to manage her expenses.
3. *Evaluate pros and cons*: Jane weighs the pros and cons of each solution, considering factors like the impact on her credit score, monthly payments, and the time it will take to pay off her debts.
4. *Regularly review and refine*: After choosing to consolidate her debt and create a budget, Jane regularly reviews her financial situation to ensure her strategies remain effective. She makes adjustments as needed to stay on track and eventually becomes debt-free.

Case Study 2: Starting a Small Business

John, a 28-year-old software developer, dreams of starting his own software development company. He faces several challenges, including securing funding, finding clients, and managing his time. He decides to apply the problem-solving skills mentioned above.

1. *Break down complex problems*: John breaks down his goal into smaller tasks, such as creating a business plan, researching funding options, and developing a marketing strategy.

2. *Identify root causes and potential solutions*: He identifies the root causes of his challenges, such as lack of business knowledge and limited networking opportunities. He explores solutions like taking business courses, attending networking events, and seeking mentorship.
3. *Evaluate pros and cons*: John weighs the pros and cons of each solution, considering factors like cost, time commitment, and potential return on investment.
4. *Regularly review and refine*: As John works towards starting his business, he continually reviews his progress and refines his strategies. He adjusts his plans based on feedback from mentors, market trends, and his own experiences, eventually establishing a successful software development company.

- *Maintaining financial flexibility*: Financial flexibility is the ability to adapt your financial plans and strategies in response to changing circumstances or unforeseen events3. To maintain financial flexibility:

  - Establish an emergency fund to cover unexpected expenses or income disruptions.
  - Regularly review and adjust your budget to accommodate changes in income or expenses.
  - Diversify your investments to minimize risk and protect against market fluctuations.

- *Leveraging your support system*: Relying on the support of others can help you cope with financial stress and overcome challenges. You can seek support from:

  - ➢ Your network of successful individuals who can provide you with insights, advice, resources, and opportunities.
  - ➢ Your mentor who can provide you with guidance, feedback, encouragement, and motivation.
  - ➢ Your family and friends who can provide you with emotional, practical, or financial support.

Some examples of people who have overcome financial challenges and setbacks by building resilience and adaptability are:

- *J.K. Rowling*: The author of Harry Potter was a single mother living on welfare when she started writing her first novel. Despite facing multiple rejections from publishers, she persevered through her hardships, and eventually, her book was accepted. Rowling has since become one of the most successful authors in history[17].

- *Dave Ramsey*: The personal finance expert was once a millionaire real estate investor who lost everything due to debt and bankruptcy. Learning from his mistakes, Ramsey rebuilt his finances by following a plan that he would later share with millions of people through his books, radio show, podcasts, courses, and events.

- *Sara Blakely*: The founder of Spanx was a salesperson with no experience in fashion or business when she conceived the idea of creating a new type of shapewear.

Despite facing obstacles such as finding a manufacturer, obtaining a patent, and convincing retailers to sell her product, Blakely overcame these challenges by being resourceful, innovative, and persistent.

By building resilience and adaptability, you can turn financial challenges and setbacks into opportunities for learning and growth. Developing these skills and strategies will help you achieve your financial goals more quickly and effectively.

C. Case Studies: Overcoming Financial Obstacles

In this section, we will share inspiring case studies of individuals who have faced significant financial challenges and setbacks but ultimately persevered and achieved financial success. These stories highlight the importance of resilience, adaptability, and a positive mindset in overcoming obstacles and attracting financial abundance.

- *Chris Gardner*: Chris Gardner was a homeless single father who faced numerous challenges on his path to becoming a successful stockbroker, investor, entrepreneur, and philanthropist. He built resilience by cultivating a growth mindset and never giving up on his goal, even when facing homelessness, long hours, and the demands of his training program. He adapted to changing circumstances by learning from his experiences and applying his skills to new opportunities[10].

- *Janice Bryant Howroyd*: Janice Bryant Howroyd overcame discrimination and racism to build a billion-dollar staffing company from scratch. She built resilience by maintaining a positive mindset and focusing on the quality of her service, even when facing challenges such as securing loans and managing cash flow. She adapted to changing markets by building relationships and innovating solutions that addressed the needs of her clients[5].

- *Sophia Amoruso*: Sophia Amoruso overcame personal and professional challenges to build a successful online fashion store and become a bestselling author and media personality. She built resilience by developing problem-solving skills that helped her overcome obstacles such as legal issues, competitors, and changing markets. She adapted to new opportunities by creating a loyal fan base and leveraging her brand to launch new ventures[2].

By learning from these case studies and building resilience and adaptability, you can turn financial obstacles into opportunities for growth and ultimately achieve financial success.

Chapter 5

Sustaining Financial Success and Creating a Lasting Legacy

A. The Importance of Long-Term Planning

A chieving financial success is an ongoing journey that requires long-term planning and commitment. To sustain your financial success and create a lasting legacy, you must continually set new goals, refine your strategies, and adapt to changing circumstances. In this section, we will discuss strategies for sustaining financial success and creating a positive impact on future generations.

B. Strategies for Sustaining Financial Success

Continual Goal-Setting and Evaluation

To sustain your financial success, it's essential to regularly review your financial goals and adjust them as needed. As you achieve your goals, set new objectives and evaluate your progress. This ongoing process helps you stay focused on your long-term vision, adapt to changing circumstances, and ensure your financial strategies remain effective. To sustain your financial success, consider the following:

- *Setting intermediate milestones to track progress and maintain motivation.* For example, if your long-term goal is to retire comfortably, set milestones such as saving a certain percentage of your income each year or reaching a specific net worth by a certain age.

- *Reflecting on your successes and learning from any setbacks or mistakes.* For example, if you invested in a stock that performed poorly, evaluate the reasons why and adjust your investment strategy accordingly.

- *Being open to exploring new investment opportunities or financial strategies.* For example, if you've been primarily investing in stocks, consider exploring real estate or alternative investments that align with your goals and risk tolerance.

- *Maintaining a diverse investment portfolio to minimize risk and maximize potential returns.* For example, diversify your portfolio by investing in a mix of stocks, bonds, and real estate, or by allocating a percentage of your investments to international markets.

Lifelong Learning and Personal Development

To sustain financial success, you must continually invest in your personal growth and development. Stay informed about new trends, opportunities, and strategies in personal finance and investing. Continuously refine your skills and knowledge to make informed decisions and seize opportunities for growth. To promote lifelong learning, consider:

- *Attending workshops, conferences, and seminars* related to personal finance and investing. For example, attend a financial planning conference or a workshop on real estate investing.

- *Reading books, articles, and blogs* on relevant topics. For example, read books on investing, financial planning, or personal development.

- *Networking with successful individuals* and learning from their experiences and insights. For example, connect with successful investors, financial planners, or entrepreneurs in your community or industry.

Staying Adaptable and Embracing Change

Financial markets and circumstances are constantly evolving. To sustain your financial success, you must stay adaptable and embrace change. This adaptability allows you to seize new opportunities and navigate challenges effectively. To stay adaptable, consider:

- *Regularly reviewing your financial strategies* and adjusting them in response to changing circumstances or market conditions. For example, if interest rates rise, adjust your investment strategy accordingly.

- *Being open to exploring new investment* opportunities or financial strategies. For example, consider investing in emerging markets or new technologies that align with your goals and risk tolerance.

- *Maintaining a diverse investment portfolio* to minimize risk and maximize potential returns. For example, diversify your portfolio by investing in a mix of stocks, bonds, and real estate, or by allocating a percentage of your investments to international markets.

C. Creating a Lasting Legacy

Financial success can provide you with the opportunity to create a lasting legacy that positively impacts future generations. To create a legacy, consider:

- *Establishing a financial plan* to support your family's future needs, such as education, healthcare, and retirement. For example, establish a trust fund for your children's education or create a healthcare fund to cover their medical expenses in case of unexpected illnesses.

- *Creating a will or trust* to ensure your assets are distributed according to your wishes. It's important to have a plan in place to ensure that your assets are distributed according to your wishes after your passing. Creating a will or trust can help you do this, and it's important to regularly update them to reflect any changes in your circumstances or wishes.

- *Engaging in philanthropy or charitable* giving to support causes you are passionate about. Giving back to the community or supporting causes you believe in can help create a positive impact beyond your immediate family. Consider donating to charities or organizations that align with your values or volunteering your time to support their efforts.

- *Sharing your financial knowledge and experiences* with younger generations, inspiring and empowering them to achieve their own financial success. By sharing your experiences and knowledge with younger generations, you can help inspire and empower them to achieve their own financial success. Consider mentoring a young person or participating in financial education programs in your community.

By focusing on long-term planning, lifelong learning, adaptability, and creating a lasting legacy, you can sustain your financial success and make a positive impact on future generations. This holistic approach to financial success will ensure that you not only achieve your own goals but also inspire and support those who come after you, ultimately becoming a true money magnet.

D. Case Studies: Sustaining Financial Success and Creating a Lasting Legacy

In this section, we will share inspiring case studies of individuals who have sustained their financial success and created a lasting legacy that positively impacted future generations. These stories highlight the importance of continual goal-setting, lifelong learning, adaptability, and giving back.

- *Andrew Carnegie*: Andrew Carnegie was a Scottish-American businessman and philanthropist who amassed a great fortune in the steel industry. He believed in the concept of "Gospel of Wealth," which held that the wealthy had a moral obligation to use their wealth to improve society. Carnegie gave away most of his wealth to support causes such as education, libraries, and peace. He also founded the Carnegie Corporation of New York, which is one of the largest charitable foundations in the world.

- *Warren Buffett*: Warren Buffett is an American investor, business magnate, and philanthropist who is widely regarded as one of the most successful investors in history. He built his wealth through astute investments and wise business decisions. Buffett is also known for his philanthropy, having pledged to give away 99% of his wealth to charity. He founded the Giving Pledge, which encourages the world's wealthiest individuals to donate the majority of their wealth to charitable causes.

- *Oprah Winfrey*: Oprah Winfrey is an American media executive, talk show host, actress, producer, and philanthropist who is one of the most influential women in the world. She built her wealth through her media empire, which includes television, film, publishing, and digital media. Winfrey is also known for her philanthropy, having donated millions of dollars to support causes such as education, healthcare, and disaster relief. She also founded the Oprah Winfrey Leadership Academy for Girls in South Africa, which provides education and leadership development to disadvantaged girls.

By following the strategies for sustaining financial success and creating a lasting legacy, you can achieve not only personal success but also contribute to the greater good. Continual goal-setting, lifelong learning, adaptability, and giving back can help you build a financial legacy that positively impacts future generations.

Journey to Fulfillment

By Melody Wallack

In the land of self-discovery, where dreams entwine,
A journey unfolds, as we learn to refine.
The steps that we take, the wisdom we share,
A dance of fulfillment, as we prioritize self-care.

With the wind at our back, a chorus of cheer,
We surround ourselves with love, as positive influences draw near.
Through the valleys of doubt, the mountains of strife,
We find strength in persistence, as we embrace life.

In the quest for wisdom, as we traverse unknown lands,
We learn to seek help, to reach out our hands.
For the beauty of growth lies in unity, in trust,
The bonds that we forge, as we rise from the dust.

With each victory earned, each milestone achieved,
We celebrate our wins, as our dreams are conceived.
Embracing patience, a virtue so grand,
We learn to walk steady, as we navigate the sand.

In the school of life, where lessons abound,
We learn from our mistakes, as wisdom is found.
Staying informed, with knowledge our guide,
We tread the path of success, as we turn the tide.

With hearts full of gratitude, we humbly reflect,
On the blessings we cherish, the love we collect.
For in this journey to fulfillment, our spirits ignite,
As we walk hand in hand, into the radiant light.

Chapter 6

Conclusion: Becoming a Money Magnet

Congratulations on taking the first step towards becoming a money magnet! You've learned about the key principles and strategies necessary for attracting financial success and creating a lasting legacy for yourself and future generations. By following these principles and tips, you can cultivate the mindset, habits, and skills necessary to achieve your financial goals.

A. Recap of Key Principles

Throughout this book, we've discussed several key principles that are essential for becoming a money magnet. These include:

- *Cultivating a Positive Mindset:* Developing an optimistic outlook, focusing on your goals, and eliminating negativity from your life to create a mental environment that fosters financial success.
- *Transformative Habits*: Adopting key financial habits such as setting clear goals, budgeting, saving and investing, and continuous learning to create a strong foundation for financial success.
- *Networking and Mentorship:* Building connections with successful individuals, nurturing your relationships, and

seeking mentorship to gain insights and opportunities that propel you towards your financial goals.

- *Overcoming Obstacles*: Cultivating resilience and adaptability to navigate challenges and setbacks on your journey to financial success.
- *Sustaining Financial Success*: Continually setting new goals, investing in personal growth, and staying adaptable to ensure long-term financial success.

B. Final Thoughts and Encouragement

As you embark on your journey to become a money magnet, remember that financial success is achievable with dedication, persistence, and the right mindset. Embrace challenges as opportunities for growth, celebrate your accomplishments, and always strive for continuous improvement. By following the principles outlined in this book, you will be well on your way to attracting financial success and creating a lasting legacy for yourself and future generations.

Now that you have the tools and strategies needed to become a money magnet, it's time to take action. Start implementing the principles and practices outlined in this book, and watch as your financial success becomes a reality. Remember, the journey may not always be easy, but with the right mindset and habits, you can overcome any obstacles that come your way and achieve the financial success you desire. Stay focused, stay positive, and keep moving forward, and you will become the money magnet you were always meant to be.

As a final note, it's important to remember that everyone's journey to financial success is unique, and what works for one person may not necessarily work for another. Therefore, it's crucial to approach your own journey with an open mind and a willingness to adapt and customize the strategies and principles outlined in this book to fit your specific needs, goals, and circumstances.

C. Additional Tips for Becoming a Money Magnet

Here are a few more ideas that can help you solidify your path to financial success:

- *Prioritize self-care*: Financial success is just one aspect of a fulfilling life. Remember to take care of your physical, mental, and emotional well-being throughout your journey. Engage in regular exercise, eat a balanced diet, maintain a healthy sleep schedule, and practice stress-reducing techniques such as meditation or mindfulness.
- *Surround yourself with positive influences:* Your environment plays a crucial role in your overall success. Surround yourself with people who uplift, inspire, and support you. Create a space that fosters productivity, creativity, and positivity.
- *Stay persistent:* Success often comes to those who persevere through setbacks and challenges. Stay committed to your goals, even when the going gets tough. Remember that setbacks are temporary, and with persistence and determination, you can overcome them and continue moving forward.

- ***Don't be afraid to ask for help***: No one achieves success alone. Reach out to friends, family, mentors, or professionals when you need advice, guidance, or support. Be open to learning from others and incorporating their insights into your journey.
- ***Celebrate your wins:*** Acknowledge and celebrate your accomplishments, both big and small. This will help you maintain motivation, boost your confidence, and reinforce the positive habits and behaviors that have led to your success.
- As you continue on your journey to becoming a money magnet, always remember that you have the power to shape your financial future. With the right mindset, habits, and strategies, you can achieve financial success and **create a lasting legacy** for yourself and future generations.
- ***Embrace patience:*** Financial success rarely happens overnight. Be prepared to invest time and effort into your journey, and understand that it may take years to fully realize your financial goals. Patience is key, and by staying focused on your long-term vision, you'll be more likely to achieve lasting success.
- ***Keep a journal:*** Documenting your journey can be a powerful tool for reflection and growth. Regularly writing about your experiences, challenges, accomplishments, and lessons learned can provide valuable insights and help you stay focused on your goals. A journal can also serve as a reminder of your progress and achievements when you need motivation or encouragement.
- ***Learn from your mistakes***: Everyone makes mistakes, but it's how you respond to them that determines your

success. Rather than dwelling on your mistakes or allowing them to hold you back, use them as opportunities to learn and grow. Reflect on what went wrong, identify areas for improvement, and apply those lessons to future decisions and actions.

- *Stay informed*: Financial markets and trends are constantly changing, and staying informed is crucial to making smart decisions and seizing opportunities. Regularly read financial news, follow industry leaders and experts, and attend events and conferences to keep up-to-date with the latest developments and insights.

- *Practice gratitude*: It's essential to maintain a grateful mindset throughout your journey to financial success. Regularly express gratitude for the opportunities, resources, and support you have, as well as the progress you've made. Practicing gratitude can help you maintain a positive mindset, stay motivated, and appreciate the journey rather than just focusing on the end goal.

- *Set Boundaries and Maintain Balance:* As you pursue financial success, it's important to maintain a healthy work-life balance. Establish boundaries to ensure that your personal and professional life don't become overly intertwined. Taking time for relaxation, hobbies, and relationships will help you stay grounded and maintain a well-rounded, fulfilling life.

- *Share Your Knowledge:* As you gain experience and expertise in your journey to financial success, consider sharing your knowledge with others. By mentoring, teaching, or writing about your experiences, you can inspire others and help them achieve their own financial goals. This act of giving back can also reinforce your own understanding and lead to personal growth.

- ***Stay True to Your Values***: Financial success should align with your personal values and beliefs. As you work towards your financial goals, stay true to your authentic self and ensure your decisions and actions reflect your values. By doing so, you'll find greater fulfillment and satisfaction in your achievements.
- ***Cultivate a Long-Term Perspective:*** Adopting a long-term perspective in your financial planning and decision-making can help you stay focused on the bigger picture. This approach can lead to more informed decisions and better outcomes, as you'll be less likely to make impulsive choices based on short-term gains or losses.

By incorporating these additional tips into your journey, you'll be better equipped to navigate the challenges and opportunities that come your way as you work towards becoming a money magnet. Remember that your journey is unique, and it's essential to stay true to yourself and your goals as you progress. With determination, persistence, and the right mindset, you can achieve the financial success you desire and create a lasting legacy for yourself and future generations.

In conclusion, becoming a money magnet is a lifelong journey that requires dedication, perseverance, and a willingness to adapt and learn. By implementing the principles and tips discussed in this book, you can create a solid foundation for financial success and ultimately attract the abundance and prosperity you desire. Remember that your journey is unique, and staying true to yourself and your goals is essential for lasting success. Good luck on your journey!

Becoming a Money Magnet

By Melody Wallack

To attract financial success,
There are habits you must possess,
A positive mindset must be formed,
Negativity must be transformed.

Set clear goals, learn to save,
Invest wisely, and always crave
Continuous growth and education,
To build a strong foundation.

Networking and mentorship,
Will provide opportunities to grip,
Gain insights from the successful,
And make your journey less stressful.

Overcoming obstacles with resilience,
Adaptability will bring brilliance,
Challenges will come, that's true,
But with persistence, you'll break through.

To sustain success, always aspire
To set new goals and never tire,
Invest in personal growth and stay agile,
To ensure long-term financial smiles.

Remember, success is not guaranteed,
Each journey is unique and customized,
But with dedication and the right mindset,
Financial success can be achieved.

Prioritize self-care, stay positive,
Surround yourself with those who uplift,
Stay persistent, don't be afraid to ask,
And always celebrate your wins at last.

Stay informed, learn from your mistakes,
Practice gratitude, for goodness sake,
Set boundaries, maintain balance and share,
Your knowledge to show that you care.

Stay true to your values, stay focused,
Adopt a long-term perspective, unprovoked,
And with dedication and persistence,
You'll become a money magnet with brilliance.

AFFIRMATIONS

- ❖ I am a magnet for financial prosperity and abundance.
- ❖ I am worthy of financial abundance and success.
- ❖ Money flows effortlessly and abundantly into my life.
- ❖ I attract positive opportunities and financial blessings.
- ❖ My financial success is inevitable and unstoppable.
- ❖ I release all limiting beliefs about money and embrace abundance.
- ❖ I am grateful for all the money and abundance in my life.
- ❖ I trust in my ability to manifest and attract financial abundance.
- ❖ I am open and receptive to all forms of financial prosperity.
- ❖ I am a successful and prosperous money magnet.
- ❖ Money flows effortlessly and easily into my life.
- ❖ I am a magnet for financial prosperity and abundance.
- ❖ I deserve to be financially successful and fulfilled.
- ❖ I am grateful for the abundance of money and resources in my life.
- ❖ My financial success grows and expands every day.

Remember to customize these affirmations to fit your specific goals and aspirations. You can also create your own affirmations based on the principles and practices outlined in the book.

THANK YOU

Dear Reader,

Thank you for taking the time to read "Money Magnet: Harness the Power of Positive Thinking and Transformative Habits to Attract Financial Success". We hope that the principles and strategies outlined in this book have been valuable in helping you cultivate the mindset and habits necessary for attracting financial success.

We believe that financial success is not only achievable but also something that should be shared with those closest to us. As such, we encourage you to share this book and the information within it with your children, family members, and friends. By doing so, you can help them build a strong foundation for their financial future and create a lasting legacy for generations to come.

Once again, we thank you for choosing "Money Magnet" and for taking the first step towards achieving financial abundance. We wish you all the best on your journey to becoming a money magnet.

Best regards,

Happy Wynn

Money, where are you?

By Melody Wallack

*M*oney, oh money, where have you gone?

I've been searching for you all day and night long

I've worked and I've toiled, I've hustled and strained

But financial freedom for me, still remains unattained

I've taken classes and coaching, gone back to school

I've worked multiple jobs, and followed every rule

But still, money seems to elude my grasp

Leaving me feeling like a failure, and in a financial rasp

*M*oney, oh money, why do you hide?

Is it because of my negative mindset and pride?

Perhaps if I switched to positive thinking and habits

I could finally reach you and relieve myself of these straits

So I'll work on myself, and on my mental game

To attract abundance and financial gain

For money, oh money, I know you're out there

And with the right mindset, I'll find you without despair.

REFERENCES

1. Allen, T. D., Eby, L. T., Poteet, M. L., Lentz, E., & Lima, L. (2004). Career benefits associated with mentoring for protégés: A meta-analysis. Journal of Applied Psychology, 89(1), 127–136. https://doi.org/10.1037/0021-9010.89.1.127
2. Amoruso, S. (2014). #Girlboss. Portfolio/Penguin.
3. Biography.com Editors. (2020). Oprah Winfrey biography. https://www.biography.com/media-figure/oprah-winfrey
4. Bogleheads Forum. (n.d.). Home. https://www.bogleheads.org/forum/index.php
5. Bryant Howroyd, J. (2017). Acting up: Winning in business and life using down-home wisdom. Center Street.
6. Buffett, W. E., & Clark, D. (2008). The Tao of Warren Buffett: Warren Buffett's words of wisdom: Quotations and interpretations to help guide you to billionaire wealth and enlightened business management. Scribner.
7. Business Networking International. (n.d.). About BNI. https://www.bni.com/about
8. Dweck, C. S. (2006). Mindset: The new psychology of success. Random House.
9. FinCon. (n.d.). Home. https://finconexpo.com/
10. Gardner, C., & Rivas, M. (2006). The pursuit of happyness. HarperCollins.
11. Invest Like a Boss Summit. (n.d.). Home. https://investlikeabosssummit.com/
12. Isaacson, W. (2011). Steve Jobs. Simon & Schuster.
13. Jonassen, D. H. (2011). Learning to solve problems: A handbook for designing problem-solving learning environments. Routledge.

14. KPMG. (2019). Advancing the future of women in business: A KPMG women's leadership summit report. https://assets.kpmg/content/dam/kpmg/us/pdf/2019/03/advancing-the-future-of-women-in-business.pdf
15. LinkedIn. (2017). How people get hired. https://business.linkedin.com/content/dam/me/business/en-us/talent-solutions/resources/pdfs/linkedin-global-recruiting-trends-2017-en-us.pdf
16. LinkedIn. (n.d.). Home. https://www.linkedin.com/
17. MoneyShow. (n.d.). Home. https://www.moneyshow.com/
18. PF Buzz. (n.d.). Home. http://pfbuzz.com/
19. Reddit Personal Finance. (n.d.). Home. https://www.reddit.com/r/personalfinance/
20. Rowling, J. K. (2008). The fringe benefits of failure, and the importance of imagination [Commencement speech]. Harvard University. https://news.harvard.edu/gazette/story/2008/06/text-of-j-k-rowling-speech/
21. Salignac, F., Marjolin, A., Reeve, R., & Muir, K. (2019). Conceptualizing and measuring financial resilience: A multidimensional framework. Social Indicators Research, 145(1), 17–38. https://doi.org/10.1007/s11205-019-02100-4
22. Stocktwits. (n.d.). Home. https://stocktwits.com/
23. The Financial Planning Association. (n.d.). Home. https://www.onefpa.org/Pages/default.aspx
24. Tip'd Finance News. (n.d.). Home. http://tipd.com/
25. Toastmasters International. (n.d.). Home. https://www.toastmasters.org/
26. Twitter. (n.d.). Home. https://twitter.com/
27. Wesabe. (n.d.). Home. https://wesabe.com/
28. Winfrey, O. (2014). What I know for sure. Flatiron Books.

Printed in Great Britain
by Amazon

23219547R00042